COURT-HOUSE AT LEXINGTON, KENTUCKY, IN 1853

ABRAHAM LINCOLN DEFENDANT

Lincoln's Most Interesting Lawsuit

BY

WILLIAM H. TOWNSEND

Of the Lexington, Kentucky, Bar

WITH ILLUSTRATIONS

THE LAWBOOK EXCHANGE, LTD.

Clark, New Jersey

2008

ISBN-13: 978-1-58477-830-1
ISBN-10: 1-58477-830-X
The quality of this reprint is equivalent to the quality of the original work.

THE LAWBOOK EXCHANGE, LTD.
33 Terminal Avenue
Clark, New Jersey 07066-1321

Please see our website for a selection of our other publications and fine facsimile reprints of classic works of legal history:
www.lawbookexchange.com

Library of Congress Cataloging-in-Publication Data

Townsend, William H. (William Henry), 1890-1964
Abraham Lincoln, defendant : Lincoln's most interesting lawsuit / William H. Townsend.
p. cm.
Originally published: Boston and New York : Houghton Mifflin Co., 1923.
The facsimiles here given are taken from the records of the Fayette Circuit court and from letters of Abraham Lincoln.
Includes bibliographical references and index.
ISBN-13: 978-1-58477-830-1 (cloth : alk. paper)
ISBN-10: 1-58477-830-X (cloth : alk. paper)
1. Lincoln, Abraham, 1809-1865--Trials, litigation, etc. 2. Oldham, Edward, 1795-1871--Trials, litigation, etc. 3. Trials (Embezzlement)--Kentucky--Lexington. I. Title.
KF228.O426T69 2007
973.7092--dc22
[B] 2007004135

Printed in the United States of America on acid-free paper

ABRAHAM LINCOLN DEFENDANT

Lincoln's Most Interesting Lawsuit

BY

WILLIAM H. TOWNSEND

Of the Lexington, Kentucky, Bar

WITH ILLUSTRATIONS

BOSTON AND NEW YORK

HOUGHTON MIFFLIN COMPANY

The Riverside Press Cambridge

1923

The Riverside Press

CAMBRIDGE · MASSACHUSETTS

PRINTED IN THE U.S.A.

Preface

LINCOLN'S most interesting lawsuit is one hitherto wholly unknown to his many biographers. In this suit, he is himself a defendant and the issue involves his own personal integrity.

Until the record was discovered among the musty files of the Fayette Circuit Court at Lexington, Kentucky, and Lincoln's letters relating thereto were unearthed from an attic where they had lain forgotten for nearly seventy years, it was believed by authorities on the subject that Lincoln had been defendant in but two lawsuits. Both of these were episodes of his struggling years at New Salem, and neither reflected in any way upon his honor, the very keystone of his character. With them the public is more or less familiar.

The first one grew out of a horse-trade.

Preface

Lincoln had purchased a horse from a man named Watkins for fifty dollars. It was agreed that payments might be made by installments, but, when only a balance of ten dollars remained, the impatient creditor sued Lincoln, who admitted the debt, borrowed the money, and paid it.

The second suit was in 1834, when one Van Bergen sought to enforce payment of a note given by the ill-fated partnership of Lincoln & Berry while in the grocery business at New Salem. Lincoln, penniless, but steadfast in his determination to pay the debts of the firm, made no defense and surrendered his horse, saddle, bridle, and surveying instruments to satisfy the judgment. Poverty alone made him a defendant in these two instances, and throughout his career as a lawyer no person, except in the case hereafter related, ever claimed that Abraham Lincoln was guilty of a dishonest act.

Preface

Henry C. Whitney, in his "Life on the Circuit with Lincoln," says of him: "His great reputation for integrity was well deserved. The most punctilious honor ever marked his professional and private life. No one ever accused him of taking an underhanded or unfair advantage in the whole course of his professional career."

In the words of Judge Davis, who knew Lincoln as few of his associates did, "he never took from a client, even when the cause was gained, more than he thought the service was worth and the client ought to pay." In fact, his companions on the circuit indignantly protested that Lincoln did not really charge what his services were worth, and cited the instance when he collected a debt of six hundred dollars due a client and deducted a fee of only three dollars and fifty cents.

That Lincoln, therefore, could have ever

been accused under oath of having collected money for a client and converting the entire amount to his own use, would be unbelievable were it not for the evidence now set forth for the first time in the succeeding pages. To preserve for posterity the authentic details of this experience is the object and purpose of this little volume.

Illustrations

Abraham Lincoln, Defendant

Abraham Lincoln, Defendant

ROBERT S. TODD, the father-in-law of Abraham Lincoln, was for many years a prominent business man of Lexington and Central Kentucky. The firm of Oldham, Todd & Company, composed of Edward Oldham, Robert S. Todd, and Thomas Hemingway, owned and operated a large cotton factory in Fayette County and its products were sold extensively in Kentucky and adjoining States.

On the sixteenth day of July, 1849, Robert S. Todd died, and thereafter the business was conducted by the surviving partners under the style of Oldham & Hemingway.

In due time, Robert S. Todd's widow qualified as administratrix and began an action in the Fayette Circuit Court to settle the rather extensive estate, including the partnership of Oldham, Todd & Company.

After much delay and considerable litigation, the settlement of the estate had been practically completed and the portions due decedent's several children ascertained and adjudged, when, on the twelfth day of May, 1853, in the Fayette Circuit Court, which held its sessions in the historic old Court-House that had echoed the voices of the Marshalls, the Breckinridges, and Henry Clay, the following petition was filed:

FAYETTE CIRCUIT COURT.

Edward Oldham and
Thomas Hemingway, surviving
partners of Oldham, Todd, & Company,
Plaintiffs.

vs: Petition.

Abraham Lincoln, Ninian
W. Edwards and George
B. Kinkead, Defendants.

The plaintiffs state they are the surviving

Edward Oldham and Thomas Hemingway surviving partners of Oldham Todd & Company—
Plaintiffs.

Fayette Circuit Court

vs

Petition

Abraham Lincoln Ninian W Edwards and George B Kinkead defendants

The plaintiffs state they are the surviving partners of Oldham Todd & Company. The old firm ~~was~~ consisting of Edward Oldham Robert S Todd & Thomas Hemingway & and Robert S Todd having departed this life on the 16th of July 1849 that Abraham Lincoln and Ninian W Edwards are indebted to them in Lincoln in the sum of $472.54 Dolls ~~and~~ for money collected for said firm and unaccounted for and Edwards in $900 freight paid for him by sd firm— Both of said defendants are non Residents of this State and live in Illinois. They state they are informed and charge the fact to be that one George B Kinkead as their attorney in fact has in his hands or will have in a few days & a large amount of money under his control and possession belonging to them the proceeds of the defendants interest it being two ~~fifths~~ of a house and lot in Lexington. That said amount then due the defendants is about $1500 Dollars which is much than sufficient to pay them their demands

They pray said amount or so much as will be sufficient to pay their debts be attached and garnisheed in the hands of

of said Trueheart to pay their debt &
be held in restraint from paying
over the same or any part of it until
the further order of this Court and
other proper relief.

R Olears

Fayette County

Thomas Hemmingway says he
believes the statements of the foregoing
petition are true T Hemingway

.. Sworn to before me by Thomas Hemmingway
the 11th day of May 1853 John F Henry J.p.f.c.

Fayette County
1st Plaintiffs state their Claims are
for money Collected by said Driscole as
their attorney and not paid over and
for money paid for said Edwards for
freight.
2nd that they are just.
3 That they ought recover $489 54
4th That the defendants are non residents
of the Commonwealth of Kentucky
T Hemingway

Sworn to before me this 11th day
of May 1853 by Thomas Hemmingway
John F Henry J.p.f.c.

partners of Oldham, Todd & Company, the old firm consisting of Edward Oldham, Robert S. Todd & Thomas Hemingway, Robert S. Todd having departed this life on the 16th day of July, 1849, and that Abraham Lincoln and Ninian W. Edwards are indebted to them, Lincoln in the sum of $472.54 Dolls. for money collected for said firm and unaccounted for and Edwards in $9.00 freight paid for him by sd. firm. Both of said defendants are non-residents of this state and live in Illinois. They state they are informed and charge the fact to be that one George B. Kinkead as their attorney in fact has in his hands or will have in a few days under his control and possession a large amount of money belonging to them, the proceeds of the defendants interest it being two sixths of a house and lot in Lexington. That said amount then due the defendants is about $1500 Dollars which is much

[more] than sufficient to pay them their demands.

They pray said amount or so much as will be sufficient to pay their debts be attached and garnisheed in the hands of said Kinkead to pay their debt and he be restrained from paying over the same or any part of it until the further order of this Court and other proper relief.

C. D. Carr.

Fayette County.

Thomas Hemingway says he believes the statements of the foregoing petition are true. T. Hemingway.

Sworn to before me by Thomas Hemingway, the 11th day of May, 1853.

John Henry, J.P.F.C.

Fayette County.

1st Plaintiffs state their claims are for money collected by said Lincoln as their

ORDER OF GENERAL ATTACHMENT.

(SECTION 246.)

Edward Oldham & Thomas Hemingway, Plaintiffs, against Abraham Lincoln & Ninian W. Edwards, Defendants. } **FAYETTE CIRCUIT COURT.** ORDER OF ATTACHMENT.

The Commonwealth of Kentucky, to the Sheriff of Fayette County:

YOU are commanded to attach and safely keep the property of the Defendants, Abraham Lincoln & Ninian W. Edwards in your county, not exempt from execution, or so much thereof as will satisfy the claim of the Plaintiffs in this action, Oldham and Hemingway for Four hundred & eighty two Dollars & 54 and Thirty Dollars, for the cost thereof; and to summon the garnishees to answer in this action on the 10th day of the next August Term of the Fayette Circuit Court; and you will make due return of this order on that day.

WITNESS: THOMAS S. REDD, Clerk of said Court, this 12 day of May, 1853.

Tho. S. Redd C. F. C. C.

(SUMMONS—ORDINARY.)

THE COMMONWEALTH OF KENTUCKY,

To the Sheriff of Fayette *County, Greeting:*

YOU ARE COMMANDED TO SUMMON Abraham Lincoln Ninian W. Edwards. & George B. Kinkead

to answer, on the first day of the next August term of the Fayette Circuit Court, a petition filed against them in said Court, by Edward Oldham and Thomas Hemingway

and warn them that, upon their failure to answer, the petition will be taken for confessed, or they will be proceeded against for contempt; and you will make due return of this summons, on the first day of the next August term of said Court.

Witness, THOMAS S. REDD, Clerk of our said Court, this 12th day of May 1853.

Tho. S. Redd
Clerk

attorney and not paid over and for money paid for said Edwards for freight.
2nd. That they are just.
3rd. That they ought to recover $481.54.
4th. That the defendants are non-residents of the Commonwealth of Kentucky.

T. HEMINGWAY.

Sworn to before me this 11th day of May, 1853, by Thomas Hemingway.

JOHN HENRY, J.P.F.C.

The first information that such a suit had been instituted, or even contemplated, evidently came to the defendants through Mr. Kinkead, who wrote them at Springfield, probably inclosing a copy of the petition, and to which letter Mr. Lincoln promptly replied:

DANVILLE, ILLS. *May* 27, 1853.

GEORGE B. KINKEAD, ESQ.,
Lexington, Ky.

I am here attending court a hundred and

thirty miles from home, and where a copy of your letter of this month, to Mr. Edwards, reached me from him, last evening. I find it difficult to suppress my indignation towards those who have got up this claim against me. I would really be glad to hear Mr. Hemingway explain how he was induced to *swear* he *believed* the claim to be just! I herewith inclose my answer. If it is insufficient either in substance, or in the authentication of the oath, return it to me at Springfield (where I shall be after about ten days) stating the defective points. You will perceive in my answer, that I ask the Petitioners to be ruled to file a bill of particulars, stating *names* & *residences* &c. I do this to enable me to absolutely disprove the claim. I can really prove by independent evidence, every material statement of my answer, and if they will name any living accessable man, as one of whom I have received their money, I will,

Danville Ills. May 27 1853

George B Kinkead, Esq
Lexington,
Ky.

I am here attending court a hundred and thirty miles from home, and where a copy of your letter of this month, to Mr. Edwards, reached me from him, last evening. I find it difficult to suppress my indignation towards those who have got up this claim against me. I would really be glad to hear Mr. Hemingway explain how he was induced to *swear*, he *believed* the claim to be just! I herewith enclose my answer. If it is insufficient either in substance, or in the authentication of the oath, return it to me at, at Springfield (where I shall be after about ten days) stating the defective points. You will perceive in my answer that I ask the Petitioners to be ruled to file a bill of particulars, stating *names* & *residences* &c. I do this to enable me to absolutely disprove the claim. I can really prove by independent evidence, every material statement of my answer; and if they will name any living accessable man, as one of whom I have received their money, I will, by *that man* disprove the charge. I know it is for *them* to prove their claim, rather than for *me* to disprove it; but I am unwilling to trust the oath of any man, who either *made* or *prompted* the oath to the Petition.

Write me soon. Very Respectfully A. Lincoln

by that man disprove the charge. I know it is for *them* to prove their claim, rather than for *me* to disprove it; but I am unwilling to trust the oath of any man, who either *made* or *prompted* the oath to the Petition.

Write me soon.

Very Respectfully,

A. LINCOLN.

The answer which was inclosed is as follows:

The separate answer of Abraham Lincoln to a Petition exhibited in the Fayette circuit court in the Commonwealth of Kentucky, against said Lincoln, Ninian W. Edwards, and George B. Kinkead, by Edward Oldham and Thomas Hemingway, sen'r, surviving partners of Oldham, Todd & Co.

This Respondent, saving, reserving &c, for answer to said Petition says he believes it is true, and therefore he admits that said Petitioners are the surviving partners of said firm of Oldham, Todd & Co; that said firm did consist of the persons named as the members thereof in said Petition; and that said Robert S. Todd did depart this life about the time stated in said Petition. But this Respondent utterly denies that he is, or ever was, indebted to said firm, or to said Petitioners as surviving partners thereof, or in any way howsoever; he denies that he ever collected $472 54/100 or any other sum whatever, for said firm, or of money belonging to said firm, or to said Petitioners, in any capacity whatever; he denies that he ever had placed in his charge for collection, any debt or claim for said firm, or for said Petitioners, of any sort whatever; and he denies that he ever was employed as the attorney or in any other capacity, of said firm, or of said Petitioners, in any matter whatever, so far as he remem-

The separate answer of Abraham Lincoln to a Petition exhibited in the Fayette circuit court in the Commonwealth of Kentucky, against said Lincoln, Ninian W. Edwards, and George B Kinkead, by Edward Oldham and Thomas Hemingway, sen: surviving partners of Oldham, Todd &co—

This Respondent, saving, reserving &c, for answer to said Petition, says he believes it is true, and therefore he admits that said Petitioners are the surviving partners of said firm of Oldham Todd &co; that said firm did consist of the persons named as the members thereof in said Petition; and that said Robert S. Todd did depart this life about the time stated in said Petition— But this Respondent utterly denies that he is, or ever was, indebted to said firm, or to said Petitioners as surviving partners thereof, or in any way howsoever; he denies that he ever collected $472.54/100 or any other sum whatever, for said firm, or of money belonging to said firm, or to said Petitioners, in any capacity whatever; he denies that he ever had placed in his charge for collection, any debt or claim, for said firm, or for said Petitioners, of any sort whatever; and he denies that he ever was employed as the attorney, or in any other capacity, of said firm, or of said Petitioners, in any matter whatever, so far as he remembers or believes— Respondent can not conceive on what the charge of said Petitioners against him is founded, unless it be the following facts— In the autumn of 1843, and after Respondent had intermarried with said Robert S. Todd's daughter, said Robert S. Todd visited Springfield, Illinois, when and where, respondent, for the first time in his life, met him—

During that visit, said Todd remarked to this Respondent that there were two desperate or doubtful debts due Oldham Todd & Co— one at, or near Beardstown, Illinois, in charge of an attorney by the name of Henry E. Dummer, and the other at Shelbyville, Illinois, in charge of whom Respondent does not remember, and that if any thing could be collected on said debts he desired Respondent to take and retain it as his own— Afterwards, and, as Respondent remembers, in 1846, said Dummer paid over to this Respondent, the sum of fifty dollars, representing that sum to be all, beyond charges, that could be collected on the said claim in his hands— And as to the said debt at Shelbyville, nothing whatever has come to the hands of this Respondent directly or indirectly; and Respondent supposes said debt has not been paid to any one else, but remains wholly unpaid— If Respondent ever knew, he has forgotten the name of the debtor at Beardstown; but he believes one Marshall Basye was the debtor, or one of the debtors, at Shelbyville— Respondent was not desired to take, and did not take charge of said claims as an attorney, or in any otherwise than as herein stated; so far as he remembers or believes he never spoke or wrote to either of the debtors on the subject, nor ever in any way attempted to ~~any~~ supersede the attornies in whose hands the claims were originally placed; and, with the exception of the fifty dollars aforesaid, received by Respondent under the circumstances foresaid, Respondent denies that he ever received any thing whatever, to which said firm, or said Petitioners could have a pretence of a claim— Respondent further states that when he visited Lexington in the Autumn of 1849, as he remembers, he stated this whole matter to said Hemingway and to L. O. Todd, as he now states it; and that, more recently, in the Spring of 1852, he again fully stated it, in his sworn answer to a Bill filed for the adjustment of the estate of said Robert S. Todd, which answer doubtless is on file in the said Fayette Circuit court, and Respondent supposes said court, in that case decided and adjusted the rights of the parties arising upon said state of facts— Respondent cares but little for said fifty dollars; if it is his legal right he prefers retaining it; but he objects to repaying it *once* to the estate of said Robert S. Todd, and *again* to said firm, or to said Petitioners; and he particularly objects to being compelled to pay money to said firm or said Petitioners which he never received at all— Respondent prays that said Petitioners may be ruled to file a Bill of particulars, stating the *names* and *residences* of the persons of whom, they claim that Respondent has collected money belonging to them— Respondent admits that he resides in Illinois; that said George B. Kinkead is his attorney; and that he had means in his hands belonging to Respondent, substantially as is in said Petition stated; and now having fully answered &c.

A. Lincoln—

State of Illinois }
Vermilion County } SS

Before me, Samuel G. Craig, clerk of the circuit court of the county aforesaid, this day personally appeared Abraham Lincoln, whose name is subscribed to the answer written on this sheet, and who being by me first duly sworn, states on oath that all the statements in said answer are true in substance and in fact— In witness whereof I have hereunto subscribed my name and affixed the seal of said court on this 27th day of May AD. 1853.

Saml G. Craig. Clk

Oldham & Hemingway
vs } Answer of Lincoln.
Lincoln & others.
Filed & Dockted June
13th 1853.
Att Sam G. Craig Clk

bers or believes. Respondent cannot conceive on what the charge of said Petitioners against him is founded, unless it be the following facts—In the autumn of 1843, and after Respondent had intermarried with said Robert S. Todd's daughter, said Robert S. Todd visited Springfield, Illinois, when and where, Respondent, for the first time in his life, met him.

During that visit, said Todd remarked to this Respondent that there were two desperate or doubtful debts due Oldham, Todd & Co — *one* at, or near, Beardstown, Illinois, in charge of an attorney by the name of Henry E. Dummer, and the other at Shelbyville, Illinois, in charge of whom Respondent does not remember, and that if any thing could be collected on said debts he desired Respondent to take and retain it as his own. Afterwards, and as Respondent remembers, in 1846, said Dummer paid over to this

Respondent, the sum of fifty dollars, representing that sum to be all, beyond charges, that could be collected on the said claim in his hands. And as to the said debt at Shelbyville, nothing whatever has come to the hands of this Respondent directly or indirectly, and Respondent supposes said debt has not been paid to any one else, but remains wholly unpaid. If Respondent ever knew, he has forgotten the name of the debtor at Beardstown; but he believes one Marshall Basye was the debtor, or one of the debtors, at Shelbyville. Respondent was not desired to take, and did not take charge of said claims as an attorney, or in any otherwise than as herein stated; so far as he remembers or believes he never spoke or wrote to either of the debtors on the subject; nor ever in any way attempted to supersede the attornies in whose hands the claims were originally placed; and, with the exception of the fifty dollars aforesaid, received by Respondent under the circumstances aforesaid, Respondent denies that he ever received any thing whatever, to which said firm, or said Petitioners could have a pretence of a claim. Respondent further states that when he visited Lexington in the autumn of 1849, as he remembers, he stated this whole matter to said Hemingway and to L. O. Todd, as he now states it; and that, more recently, in the spring of 1852, he again fully stated it, in his sworn answer to a Bill filed for the adjustment of the estate of said Robert S. Todd, which answer doubtless is on file in the said Fayette circuit court, and Respondent supposes said court, in that case, decided and adjusted the rights of the parties arising upon said state of facts.

Respondent cares but little for said fifty dollars; if it is his legal right he prefers retaining it; but he objects to repaying it *once* to the estate of said Robert S. Todd, and *again* to said firm or to said Petitioners; and he particularly objects to being compelled to pay money to said firm or said Petitioners which he never received at all.

Respondent prays that said Petitioners may be ruled to file a Bill of particulars, stating the *names* and *residences* of the persons of whom, they claim that Respondent has collected money belonging to them. Respondent admits that he resides in Illinois; that said George B. Kinkead is his attorney; and that he had means in his hands belonging to Respondent, substantially as is in said Petition stated; and now having fully answered &c.

A. LINCOLN.

STATE OF ILLINOIS }
} SS
VERMILION COUNTY }

Before me, Samuel G. Craig, clerk of the

Circuit Court of the County aforesaid, this day personally appeared Abraham Lincoln, whose name is subscribed to this answer written on this sheet, and who being by me first duly sworn, states on oath that all the statements in said answer are true in substance and in fact. In witness whereof I have hereunto subscribed my name and affixed the seal of said Court on this 27th day of May, A.D. 1853.

SAM'L G. CRAIG, *Clk.*

The Fayette Circuit Court was not then a court of continuous session, but held terms of several weeks in February, June and August of each year.

Although the summons did not require Lincoln to answer until the first day of the next August term, it will be noticed that he prepared his statement of defense within twenty-four hours after receiving information that suit had been instituted and, on the first day of the June term, which convened on Monday, June 13, 1853, his answer was duly filed in the Fayette Circuit Court.

To the defense presented by Lincoln's answer, the plaintiffs filed no reply and the issue being thus joined, under the practice, the case stood for trial during the June Term. It appears, however, that Oldham & Hemingway made no effort to have the case assigned for hearing, although Court did not adjourn until the twenty-fifth day of June.

After adjournment, nothing having been done and the matter evidently weighing considerably on his mind, Lincoln wrote his lawyer again.

SPRINGFIELD, ILLS.
July 6, 1853.

GEO. B. KINKEAD, ESQ.
Lexington, Ky.
DEAR SIR:

I feel some anxiety about the suit which

Springfield, Ills. July 6. 1853.

Geo. B. Kinkead Esq
Lexington, Ky.

Dear Sir:

I feel some anxiety about the suit which has been gotten up against me in your court; and I therefore hope you will pardon my requesting you to write me when your court sits— whether it is probable I shall have to take proof here &c. &c— In the autumn of 1849 I was at Lexington several days, during which time I was almost constantly with L. O. Todd; and, if he shall, when the case comes on to be tried, *think* he *remembers* that I told him I had collected money for Oldham Todd & Co, the story would be plausable enough to require an answer— Such recollection would be an utter mistake; yet if something of the sort is not relied on, I can not not conceive how Mr Hemingway was induced to swear to the truth of the Bill, for they can not, in any other way make the slightest show of proof. I therefore think it safest to look to their making this proof, as, at least, possible, so as to be prepared for it— I have said before, and now repeat, that if they will name the man or men of whom, they say, I have collected money for them, I will disprove it— I hope you will write me at once— I conclude with the remark that I expect you to be compensated for your services in this case, in addition, to your compensation for your attention to our business in common there—

Respectfully

A. Lincoln—

has been gotten up against me in your court; and I therefore hope you will pardon my requesting you to write me when your court sits — whether it is probable I shall have to take proof here &c, &c. In the autumn of 1849 I was at Lexington several days, during which time I was almost constantly with L. O. Todd; and if he shall, when the case comes on to be tried, *think* he *remembers* that I told him I had collected money for Oldham, Todd & Co, the story would be plausable enough to require an answer. Such recollection would be an utter mistake; yet if something of the sort is not relied on, I can not conceive how Mr. Hemingway was induced to swear to the truth of the Bill; for they can not in any other way make the slightest show of proof. I therefore think it safest to look to their making this proof, as, at least, possible, and to be prepared for it. I have said before, and now repeat, that if they will name the man or men of whom, they say, I have collected money for them, I will *disprove* it. I hope you will write me at once. I conclude with the remark that I expect you to be compensated for your services in this case, in addition to your compensation for your attention to our business, in common, there.

Respectfully, A. LINCOLN.

It is evident that, from the beginning, Lincoln had been aware of a certain influence, not exactly in the open, which he thought was largely responsible for this litigation. This is indicated by the reference in his letter of May 27th, to the "man who either made or prompted the oath to the Petition." It now becomes apparent that the person whom Lincoln suspected as having "prompted the oath" was none other than his brother-in-law, Levi O. Todd.

The Todd estate had just been wound up and not without friction among some of the heirs. The record of the settlement suit discloses considerable ill-feeling between Levi O. Todd and his sisters, Mary Lincoln, Frances Wallace, and Ann Smith, who lived in Springfield, growing out of advancements which Todd claimed his father had made during his lifetime to these children and particularly to Mary Lincoln. No doubt these facts were in Lincoln's mind when he wrote the above letter to Mr. Kinkead.

In reply to this letter, Mr. Kinkead must have informed Lincoln that plaintiffs did not intend to prosecute the case further. He probably thought that the answer had convinced them of their error. Yet, when on the second day of August, Court again convened and plaintiffs made no motion for dismissal, Mr. Kinkead wrote his clients the day before Court adjourned on September

3d. To this letter, Lincoln responded as follows:

BLOOMINGTON, ILLS.
Sept. 13, 1853.

GEO. B. KINKEAD, ESQ.
Lexington, Ky.

DEAR SIR: —

Your letter of the 2nd inst to Mr. Edwards, has been forwarded by him to me here where I am attending court. When, in your letter to me, of the 12th July, you gave the opinion that O. T. & Co would abandon their suit, it was plain to my mind they intended no such thing, else they would have told you so plainly. The matter now takes me at great disadvantage, in this, that it will cost me more to leave the Circuit (which has just commenced) and attend to taking proof, than it would to give up the claim; and your letter does not mention the *time* of your next term.

Bloomington, Ills. Sept. 13. 1853.

Geo. B. Kinkead, Esq

Lexington, Ky-

Dear Sir:

Your letter of the 2nd. Inst. to Mr. Edwards, has been forwarded by him to me here where I am attending court- When, in your letter to me, of the 12th. July, you gave the opinion that O. T. Hos would abandon their suit, it was plain to my mind they intended no such thing, else they would have told you so plainly. The matter now takes me at great disadvantage, in this, that it will cost me more to leave the Circuit (which has just commenced) and attend to taking proof, than it would to give up the claim; and your letter does not mention the *time* of your next term-

But the great difficulty of all is the want of something definite, to take proof about- Without a bill of particulars

stating the names of the persons of whom,
O. T. & Co. claim that I have collected
money for them, any proof I can possibly
take, will be wide of the mark— can
not meet Levi's statement, (which I now
suppose he is determined to make) that "I
told him I owed the amount attached"—
I can prove by John T. Stuart, of Spring
field Illinois, that he & I were partners
in the law from the Spring of 1837 to
the Spring of 1841, and that, so far as
he knows, we never had any business for
O. T. & Co— By ~~Ninian W. Edwards~~ Stephen
T. Logan of Springfield, Ills, that he
& I were partners from the Spring of 1841
to the autumn of 1844, and that so far
as he knows, he & I never had any busin
ess for O. T. & Co— By William H. Herndon
of Springfield, Ills, that he & I have been
partners from the autumn of 1844 up to
the present time, and that so far as
he knows, he & I never had any business
for O. T. & Co— and by all three that

they never knew of me, individually, having any business for O. T. Co— Also, by Ninian W. Edwards, of Springfield, Ills, that so far as he knows, or believes, the whole of the business of O. T. Co in Illinois passed through his hands, and that so far as he knows or believes, none of it ever went into my hands— that the claims at Beardstown & Shelbyville both passed through his hands, and were, in the fall of 1843, given to me, as desparate debts, by Mr. Todd, in manner as I have stated in my answer; and that less than three years ago, the father-in-law of one of the debtors, called on him to try to compound the debt— As I understand, both these claims went into judgments; and as to that at Beardstown, I can prove the truth of the answer, by the record, and by Henry E Dummer of Beardstown, Cass Co Ills— As to that at Shelbyville, I can prove the truth of the answer, by the record that it was taken not by me, but by a different attorney; and that it remains apparently unsatisfied— By William F. Thornton of Shelbyville, Illinois, that he is the father-in-law of the debtor— that the debtor has gone to California; and that he left this, among others, as an unpaid debt, which he desired the witness to compound for him if he could.

All this I can prove; but without a Bill of particulars, it seems to me, it will not meet the case— *Can they not be ruled to give a Bill of particulars?*

This matter harrasses my feelings a good deal; and I shall be greatly obliged if you will write me immediately, under *cover to Mr Edwards* at Springfield Ills— telling me first, when is the next term of your court; and second, whether I *can* or can *not* have a bill of particulars—

Yours truly

A. Lincoln

But the great difficulty of all is the want of something definite, to take proof about. Without a bill of particulars stating the names of the persons of whom, O. T. & Co claim that I have collected money for them, any proof I can possibly take, will be wide of the mark — can not meet Levi's statement, (which I now suppose he is determined to make) that "I told him I owed the amount attached." I can prove by John T. Stuart, of Springfield, Illinois, that he & I were partners in the law from the Spring of 1837 to the Spring of 1841, and that, so far as he knows, we never had any business for O. T. & Co. By Stephen T. Logan of Springfield, Ills., that he and I were partners from the Spring of 1841 to the autumn of 1844, and that so far as he knows, he & I never had any business for O. T. & Co. By William H. Herndon of Springfield, Ills., that he & I have been partners from the autumn of 1844 up to the present time; and that so far as he knows, he & I never had any business for O. T. & Co — and by all three, that they never knew of me, individually, having any business for O. T. & Co. Also, by Ninian W. Edwards of Springfield, Ills., that so far as he knows or believes the whole of the business of O. T. & Co. in Illinois passed through his hands, and that so far as he knows or believes, none of it ever went into my hands — that the claims at Beardstown & Shelbyville both passed through his hands and were, in the fall of 1843, given to me, as desperate debts, by Mr. Todd, in manner as I have stated in my answer; and that less than three years ago, the father-in-law of one of the debtors called on him to try to compound the debt. As I understand, both these claims went into judgments, and as to that at Beardstown, I can prove the truth of the answer, by the record, and by Henry E. Dummer of Beardstown, Cass Co., Ills. As to that at Shelbyville, I can prove the truth of the answer, by the record that it was taken, not by me, but by a different attorney; and that it remains apparently unsatisfied. By William F. Thornton of Shelbyville, Illinois, that he is the father-in-law of the debtor — that the debtor has gone to California; and that he left this, among others, as an unpaid debt, which he desired the witness to compound for him if he could. All this I can prove; but without a Bill of particulars, it seems to me, it will not meet the case. *Can they not be ruled to give a Bill of particulars?*

This matter harrasses my feelings a good deal; and I shall be greatly obliged if you will write me immediately, *under cover to Mr. Edwards at Springfield*, Ills—telling me first, *when* is the next term of your court; and second, whether I *can* or can *not* have a bill of particulars.

Yours truly,

A. LINCOLN.

Apparently at this time, Lincoln and his attorney were both unaware that plaintiffs had already filed an exhibit which doubtless was intended as a bill of particulars. This exhibit, filed August 10th, is a statement of account as follows:

To Claims sent A. Lincoln for Collection.	
1841	
June 17. H. E. Dummer — Blain, Tompkins & Barrett Claim, amt	$129.05
1843	
Dec 8 Amt of claim on Hawley & Edwards for cotton yarns sent them for sale, proceeds.	$343.49
	$472.54

Under the pleadings, the burden of proof was on the plaintiffs and, as Lincoln aptly observed, it was not his duty first to disprove the allegations of the petition. No doubt, a motion to dismiss for want of prosecution would have been sustained by the Court, but this was not Lincoln's way of winning the suit. He would not rely on technicalities when his honor and integrity had been assailed. The record must show a complete refutation of the charge. Since no effort had been made by plaintiffs to obtain a trial during the June and August terms, it was necessary for Lincoln to assume the burden of proof which he did on September 22, 1853, by having the following notice to plaintiffs issued through his attorney:

Messrs. Oldham & Hemingway, survivors of Oldham, Todd & Co.

Gentlemen:

Take notice that I will take depositions to be read by me in the suit now pending in the Fayette Circuit Court, wherein you are plaintiffs & I am defendant with others, at the following times & places, to-wit: At the office of the Clerk of the Circuit Court of Sangamon County, Illinois, in Springfield on the 12 day of Nov'r next, at which place I will take the deposition of I. T. Stewart & others — At the office of the Clerk of the Cass Circuit Court in the town of Beardstown, County of Cass, State of Illinois, on the 15th of Nov'r, 1853, at which place I will take the deposition of H. E. Dummer & others — At the office of the Clerk of the Circuit Court of Shelby County in the town of Shelbyville, in said County, State of Illinois, on the 8th of Nov'r, 1853, at which place I will take the depositions of William F. Thornton & others —

ABM. LINCOLN.

Sep. 22, 1853.

This notice was duly served as the official return shows:

"Messrs Oldham & Hemingway survivors of Oldham Todd &co.

Gentleman

Take notice that I will take depositions to be read by me in the suit now pending in the Fayette Circuit Court wherein you are plaintiffs & I am defendant with others, at the following times & places, towit; At the office of the Clerk of the Circuit Court of Sangamon County, Illinois, in Springfield on the 12 day of Novr next, at which place I will take the deposition of J. T. Stewart & others— At the office of the Clerk of the Cass Circuit Court in the town of Beardstown, county of Cass, State of Illinois, on the 15th of Novr 1853 at which place I will take the deposition of H. E. Dummer & others— At the office of the Clerk of the Circuit Court of Shelby County in the town of Shelbyville, in said County, state of Illinois, on the 8th of Novr 1853, at which place I will take the depositions of William F. Thornton & others—

Sep. 22. 1853— Abm Lincoln"

"Executed September 23rd 1853— By delivering to Thomas Hemingway & Edward Oldham each a true copies of the within notice—

John Rodes DS
for Waller Rodes S/c"

The Deposition of Anthony Thornton Esq, taken in pursuance of a written notice and entry of service indorsed on the back thereof, of which notice, and entry of service, the foregoing are true copies, and the originals of which are retained by the defendant, to be used

"Messrs Oldham & Hemingway, survivors of Oldham, Todd & Co
Gentlemen

Take notice that I will take depositions to be read by me in the suit now pending in the Fayette Circuit Court, wherein you are plaintiffs & I am Defendant with others, at the following times and places towit: At the office of the Clerk of the Circuit court of Sangamon County, Illinois, in Springfield, on the 12 day of Novr. next, at which place I will take the deposition of J. T. Stewart & others—

At the office of the Clerk of the Cass Circuit Court in the town of Beardstown, County of Cass, State of Illinois, on the 15th of Novr. 1853, at which place I will take the deposition of H. E. Dummer & others—

At the office of the Clerk of the Circuit court of Shelby county, in the town of Shelbyville in said county, State of Illinois, on the 8th of Novr. 1853, at which place I will take the deposition, of William F. Thornton & others— Sept. 22-1853— Abm- Lincoln"

"Executed, September 23rd 1853, by delivering to Thomas Hemingway & Edward Oldham, each true copies of the within notice—

John Rodes D.S.
for Waller Rodes S/C"

Deposition of Ninian W. Edwards & Eliphalet B Hawley——

——taken before me, William F. Elkin, and acting Justice of the Peace, in and for the County of Sangamon and State of Illinois, in pursuance of a written notice, of which, and of the entry of service thereof, the above, are true copies, and the original of which is retained by the defendant, to be used

Executed, September 23rd, 1853, by delivering to Thomas Hemingway & Edward Oldham, each true copies of the within notice. JOHN RODES, D.S.
for WALLER RODES, S.F.C.

In the mean time, having been apprised as to the exhibit or statement of account, Lincoln wrote his attorney again:

PEORIA, ILLS. *Sept.* 30, 1853.

GEO. B. KINKEAD, ESQ.
Lexington, Ky.

DEAR SIR:

Your letter of the 22nd has just reached me through Mr. Edwards; and for which I thank you heartily. I now feel that the case is entirely manageable. I well know who Hawley and Edwards are. The "Hawley" of that firm is Eliphalet B. Hawley; and the "Edwards" is no other than Ninian W. Edwards, whom you know nearly as well as I do, & being the same who, on behalf of himself, and the rest of us here, has conducted all the business with you, in relation to Mr. Todd's estate. Mr. Hawley still lives at Springfield; and I will thank you to give a notice to take his deposition at the same time and place named in my former letter for the taking of that of Mr. Edwards & others at Springfield.

Very truly yours &c.

A. LINCOLN.

P. S. Still write me, under cover to Mr. Edwards at Springfield, who will forward to me. A. L.

On the dates fixed in this notice Lincoln took the following testimony, the captions of all the depositions being entirely in his handwriting:

The deposition of Anthony Thornton of Shelbyville, Illinois, states that deponent is a practicing attorney at law in Shelbyville

Peoria Ills Sept. 30 1853

Geo. B. Kinkead, Esq

Lexington, Ky.

Dear Sir

Your letter of the 23rd has just reached me through Mr. Edwards, and for which I thank you heartily — I now feel that the case is entirely managable — I well know who Hawley and Edwards are — The "Hawley" of that firm is Eliphalet B. Hawley; and the "Edwards" is no other than Ninian W. Edwards, whom you know nearly as well as I do, & being the person who, on behalf of himself, and the rest of us here, has conducted all the business with you, ~~has~~, in relation to Mr Todd's estate. Mr Hawley still lives at Springfield; and I will thank you to give a notice to take his deposition at the same time and place named in my former letter for the taking of that of Mr. Edwards & others, at Springfield —

Very truly Yours, &c

A. Lincoln —

P.S. Still write me, under cover to Mr. Edwards, at Springfield, who will forward to me —

A. L.

and has been so engaged for about sixteen years; that he knew the firm of Thornton & Basye, formerly doing business at that place and that in the latter part of 1841, or beginning of 1842, Rankin & Edwards of Springfield placed in deponent's hands for collection a note, dated March 7, 1840, executed by Thornton & Basye to Rankin & Edwards for $597.00, due nine months from date; that said note is now in his possession and has been all the time since it was placed with him for collection. He states that he had been able to collect on this note only $45.00, five of which he retained as a fee and the balance of $40.00 he had turned over to N. W. Edwards of the firm of Rankin & Edwards; that suit was never instituted on said note because Thornton until the time of his death had been wholly insolvent and that Basye had no property subject to execution from 1841 to 1849, at which time he went to California permanently to live; and that William F. Thornton, father-in-law of Basye and who is absent from the State at the time this deposition is taken, had attempted to compound the debt. Deponent is "certain the defendant Lincoln has never had anything to do with said note."

The deposition of Ninian W. Edwards of Springfield states that Robert S. Todd, one of the firm of Oldham, Todd & Co., placed in the hands of Rankin & Edwards, of which firm deponent was a member, cotton yarns to sell on credit or for cash for said Oldham, Todd & Co.; that on March 7th, 1840, they sold to Thornton & Basye, of Shelbyville, Illinois, cotton yarns amounting to $597.00, for which the purchaser's note was taken, due in nine months. He states that the note was held until the latter part of 1841 or the beginning of 1842, when it was placed in the hands of Anthony Thornton, a lawyer of Shelbyville, for collection; that the collection of forty dollars made by Thornton and received by deponent on April 14, 1842, was paid for Robt. S. Todd on a note executed by Todd to Nathaniel A. Ware; that sometime thereafter, Robert S. Todd had told deponent that he had given to A. Lincoln "what he could make out of said debt" and had also informed him that he had given Lincoln a debt in the hands of H. E. Dummer of Beardstown; that neither the deponent nor any member of his firm, so far as he knows, ever paid Lincoln any money whatever belonging to Oldham, Todd & Co., and that he had examined the books of the firm which showed no entry of any such payment. So far as he knows or believes Lincoln never received any money on the Thornton, Basye note at Shelbyville, as debtors were insolvent from the beginning of 1842. Deponent states that he is a defendant in the same suit with Lincoln, but in a "distinct claim" and has "no interest whatever in the claim on which said Lincoln is sued."

The deposition of Eliphalet B. Hawley of Springfield, states that deponent is a member of the firm of Hawley & Edwards, successors to Rankin & Edwards, and had been a clerk in the old firm prior to buying Mr. Rankin out in 1841; that he knew the defendant Lincoln personally and the Oldham, Todd Company of Lexington, Ky. by reputation; that he had heard the deposition of N. W. Edwards read and that his statements therein as to the Shelbyville debt were correct; and that neither he nor his firm, nor any other person, so far as he knew, had ever paid Lincoln "any money belonging to said Oldham, Todd & Co. on any account whatever."

Abraham Lincoln, Defendant

The deposition of Henry E. Dummer of Beardstown, Illinois, states that he has been a practicing attorney at that place since 1837; that he had been slightly acquainted with Robert S. Todd and had known the defendant Lincoln for many years; that Mr. Todd had placed in his hands for collection a note dated May 28, 1841, executed by Robert Lindsey to Oldham, Todd & Co. in the sum of $134.21, due one day after date; that he sued on said note and obtained judgment thereon Oct. 12, 1841, in the Cass Circuit Court; that Lindsey was in "desperate circumstances as to his pecuniary affairs" and that deponent was able to realize on said judgment in 1845, only the sum of $50.00, which was obtained through the sale of a title bond belonging to Lindsey; that, as directed by Robert S. Todd, deponent paid the $50.00 to A. Lincoln in 1846; that his recollection of the amount is clear and distinct and that nothing further was ever paid on said debt, Lindsey dying at Beardstown in August, 1846, utterly insolvent. He states positively that this is the only claim he ever had in his hands at any time belonging to the said Oldham, Todd & Co.

These four depositions, constituting the proof for the defendant and fully supporting the allegations of Lincoln's answer, were filed in the Fayette Circuit Court on the twenty-third day of November, 1853, and on January 16, 1854, plaintiffs filed a motion to dismiss the case, which was done at their cost, on February 10, 1854, when the next term began.

Lincoln's last two letters to Mr. Kinkead on this subject illustrate that generous quality of mind and heart which made him so deeply sensible of every obligation.

Abraham Lincoln, Defendant

SPRINGFIELD, ILLS.
March 31, 1854.

MR. GEORGE B. KINKEAD, ESQ.

DEAR SIR:

Your note of January 1st, informing me that Messrs. Oldham & Hemingway had dismissed their suit against me, was duly received. I write this now merely to say that I expect and desire you to be paid a separate fee for your attention to that suit; and to authorize you to retain what you shall deem reasonable on that account, out of any money of mine which is or may come into your hands. If nothing further for me is, or is likely to be in your hands, write me and I will forward you the amount.

Very truly yours &c.,

A. LINCOLN.

Abraham Lincoln, Defendant

SPRINGFIELD, ILLS.
June 16, 1854.

GEORGE B. KINKEAD,
Lexington, Ky.

DEAR SIR:—

Your letter of the 8th inst, to N. W. Edwards, enclosing a draft of between two and three hundred dollars (I write from memory only as to the amount) reached me here a day or two since, and was, in Mr. Edwards' absence, taken from the P. Office and opened by his brother. It was shown to me this morning and will be kept at the store of which Mr. Edwards is a partner until his return, which will be about six weeks hence & when, doubtless, he will write you.

I ran my eye over the contents of your letter & only have to say you do not seem to compensate yourself very liberally for the separate service you did for me.

Yours truly, A. LINCOLN.

Thus the most vexatious experience of Lincoln's picturesque career as a lawyer came to an end. Complete vindication was his. The charge of dishonesty and professional misconduct, which must have cut deeply the sensitive soul of that tall, gaunt man who long ago had earned the sobriquet of "Honest Abe," was silenced forever. And in the calm, dignified, yet prompt and vigorous defense of his own good name one may catch a glimpse of the abiding faith that "right makes might" which saved the Union and made the name of Abraham Lincoln immortal.

APPENDIX

NINIAN W. EDWARDS married Elizabeth Todd, oldest sister of Mary Todd Lincoln. It was while on a visit to this sister at Springfield that Mary Todd met Abraham Lincoln and at the Edwards home they were married on the evening of November 4, 1842. Probably no other man knew Lincoln so long and so intimately as did Ninian W. Edwards. His answer filed in the lawsuit in which he was a co-defendant with Lincoln may be of interest.

FAYETTE CIRCUIT COURT
STATE OF KENTUCKY.

Edward Oldham & Thos. Hemingway,
Surviv'g partners of
Oldham, Todd & Co. } Plaintiffs.

vs.

Abraham Lincoln &
Ninian W. Edwards } Defendants.

The Respondent, Ninian W. Edwards, being duly sworn in answer to the Plaintiffs petition states according to his best recollection, that the plaintiffs never did pay for the defendant the sum of $9. or any other sum for freight, for the use or benefit, or by the request of said Respondent for the benefit of any one else, nor did this Respondent ever know that said Plaintiffs had any such charge against him — that he is confident he never requested said plaintiffs or either of them to make said payment for him. This Respondent demands of said Plaintiffs a bill of particulars showing the date and for what purpose said money was paid.

This Respondent by way of further answer, copies the following extract of a letter bearing date Aug. 15th, 1840, and written by R. S. Todd one of the partners at that time of Oldham, Todd & Co.

"I have this day forwarded to Heran & Lees of Louisville 5 bales cotton yarns cont'g 280 doz each, which I have directed to forward to your care. I design 3 of those bales for the benefit of my daughter Frances Wallace and 2 for the benefit of Mary from whom I rec'd a letter this morning dated at Columbia, Mo: You can defray the charges of transportation from Louisville (to which place I have paid it) and charge them for it to your place."

These bales of cotton were the only articles according to this Respondent's recollection,

Fayette Circuit Court State of Kentucky.

Edward Oldham & Thos. Hemingway surviving partners of Oldham Todd & Co } Plaintiffs

v

Abraham Lincoln & Ninian W Edwards } Defendants.

This Respondent Ninian W Edwards being duly sworn in answer to the Plaintiffs petition states according to his best recollection, that the plaintiffs never did pay for these defendants the sum of $[illegible], or any other sum of money, for the use or benefit, or by request of said Respondents for the benefit of any one else, nor did this Respondent ever know that said Plaintiffs had any such charge against him. that he is confident he never requested said Plaintiffs or either of them to make said payment for him. This Respondent demands of said Plaintiffs a bill of particulars showing the date and for what purpose said money was paid.

This Respondent by way of further answer copies the following extract of a letter bearing date Aug. 15th 1840, and written by R. S. Todd one of the partners at that time of Oldham Todd & co — "I have this day forwarded to Keenon & Lees of Louisville 5 bales Cotton Yarns containing 280 doz each, which I have directed to forward to your care. I design 3 of those bales for the benefit of my daughter Frances Wallace and 2 for the benefit of Mary from whom I rec'd a letter this morning dated at Columbia Mo: You can defray the charges of transportation from Louisville (to which place I have paid it) and charge them for it to your place!! These Bales of Cotton were the only articles according to this Respondent's recollection, that were directed to him by either of said firm from Lexington, that he disposed of the same according to the directions of said R. S Todd for the benefit of said Frances & Mary. Sisters of the wife of this Respondent.

Ninian W Edwards.

State of Illinois }
City of Springfield } ss

I Thomas G Taylor Commissioner of the State of Kentucky to take the acknowledgment of Deeds and other writings duly appointed and commissioned by the Governor thereof do certify that the foregoing answer of Ninian W Edwards was this day presented to me in my office Springfield by the said Ninian W Edwards and the said Edwards subscribed and made oath to the said answer which is hereby certified and this certificate is in accordance with the instructions of the Governor of the State of Kentucky

Given under my hand this 23d day of May A.D. 1853

Thomas G. Taylor Commissioner

that were directed to him by either of said firm from Lexington; that he disposed of the same according to the directions of said R. S. Todd for the benefit of said Frances & Mary, sisters of the wife of this Respondent.

NINIAN W. EDWARDS.

STATE OF ILLINOIS } ss
CITY OF SPRINGFIELD }

I, Thomas G. Taylor, Commissioner of the State of Kentucky to take the acknowledgement of Deeds and other writings duly appointed and commissioned by the Governor thereof do certify that the foregoing answer of Ninian W. Edwards was this day presented to me in my office in Springfield by the said Ninian W. Edwards and the said Edwards subscribed and made oath to the said answer which is hereby certified and this certificate is in accordance with the instructions of the Governor of the State of Kentucky.

Given under my hand this 23rd day of May, A.D. 1853.

THOMAS G. TAYLOR,
Commissioner.

Key Words — Standard welding terminology, welding definitions, brazing, soldering, thermal spraying, thermal cutting

ANSI/AWS A3.0-94
An American National Standard

Approved by
American National Standards Institute
May 23, 1994

Standard Welding Terms and Definitions

Supersedes A3.0-89

Prepared by
AWS Committee on Definitions and Symbols

Under the Direction of
AWS Technical Activities Committee

Approved by
AWS Board of Directors

Abstract

This standard is a glossary of the technical terms used in the welding industry. Its purpose is to establish standard terms to aid in the communication of welding information. Since it is intended to be a comprehensive compilation of welding terminology, nonstandard terms used in the welding industry are also included. All terms are either standard or nonstandard. They are arranged in the conventional dictionary letter-by-letter alphabetical sequence.

A total of 1253 terms are defined, and the definitions are illustrated by 53 figures.

Also included are the Master Chart of Welding and Allied Processes and the Joining Method Chart with corollary classification charts.

American Welding Society
550 N.W. LeJeune Road, Miami, Florida 33126

Statement on Use of AWS Standards

All standards (codes, specifications, recommended practices, methods, classifications, and guides) of the American Welding Society are voluntary consensus standards that have been developed in accordance with the rules of the American National Standards Institute. When AWS standards are either incorporated in, or made part of, documents that are included in federal or state laws and regulations, or the regulations of other governmental bodies, their provisions carry the full legal authority of the statute. In such cases, any changes in those AWS standards must be approved by the governmental body having statutory jurisdiction before they can become a part of those laws and regulations. In all cases, these standards carry the full legal authority of the contract or other document that invokes the AWS standards. Where this contractual relationship exists, changes in or deviations from requirements of an AWS standard must be by agreement between the contracting parties.

International Standard Book Number: 0-87171-305-5

American Welding Society, 550 N.W. LeJeune Road, Miami, FL 33126

Printed in the United States of America

Reprinted: June 1998

Note: The primary purpose of AWS is to serve and benefit its members. To this end, AWS provides a forum for the exchange, consideration, and discussion of ideas and proposals that are relevant to the welding industry and the consensus of which forms the basis for these standards. By providing such a forum, AWS does not assume any duties to which a user of these standards may be required to adhere. By publishing this standard, the American Welding Society does not insure anyone using the information it contains against any liability arising from that use. Publication of a standard by the American Welding Society does not carry with it any right to make, use, or sell any patented items. Users of the information in this standard should make an independent, substantiating investigation of the validity of that information for their particular use and the patent status of any item referred to herein.

With regard to technical inquiries made concerning AWS standards, oral opinions on AWS standards may be rendered. However, such opinions represent only the personal opinions of the particular individuals giving them. These individuals do not speak on behalf of AWS, nor do these oral opinions constitute official or unofficial opinions or interpretations of AWS. In addition, oral opinions are informal and should not be used as a substitute for an official interpretation.

This standard is subject to revision at any time by the AWS Committee on Definitions and Symbols. It must be reviewed every five years and if not revised, it must be either reapproved or withdrawn. Comments (recommendations, additions, or deletions) and any pertinent data that may be of use in improving this standard are requested and should be addressed to AWS Headquarters. Such comments will receive careful consideration by the AWS Committee on Definitions and Symbols and the author of the comments will be informed of the Committee's response to the comments. Guests are invited to attend all meetings of the AWS Committee on Definitions and Symbols to express their comments verbally. Procedures for appeal of an adverse decision concerning all such comments are provided in the Rules of Operation of the Technical Activities Committee. A copy of these Rules can be obtained from the American Welding Society, 550 N.W. LeJeune Road, Miami, FL 33126.

Photocopy Rights